Original title:
Into the Forest We Rhyme

Copyright © 2025 Creative Arts Management OÜ
All rights reserved.

Author: Colin Leclair
ISBN HARDBACK: 978-1-80567-301-9
ISBN PAPERBACK: 978-1-80567-600-3

The Haiku of Hushed Tread

Squirrels hold a chat,
Wondering who's the spy.
Footsteps soft as mist,
Who made that shifty sigh?

Rabbits make a dash,
Hiding from the tall grass.
Sneaky birds just laugh,
Life's a silly class.

Twilight Tales of the Timberland

Moonlit shadows dance,
Bears wear pjs for fun.
Owls hoot secret songs,
While fireflies just run.

Creepy crawlers chat,
Gossip on the damp ground.
Watch out for the frogs,
Their jokes are quite profound.

Sonic Secrets of the Sylva

Echoes from the brook,
Fish just laugh and tease.
Crickets hold the mic,
While dancing with the breeze.

A raccoon steals snacks,
His friends cheer and applaud.
Nature's stand-up show,
We're the critters' squad!

Musings in the Meadow

Butterflies all giggle,
Tickling flowers' heads.
Bees buzz in a choir,
As every bloom spreads.

Grasshoppers jump high,
Chasing sunbeams of gold.
Each leap's a new tale,
Nature's joys unfold.

Rhymes of the Rustling Foliage

Leaves giggle as they sway,
Squirrels play hide and seek all day.
A bird sings off-key in a tree,
While beetles dance, so wild and free.

Rabbits hop with a funny grace,
Chasing shadows, they quicken their pace.
A fox wears a top hat, so grand,
In this whimsical, wacky land.

The Poetry of Emerging Ferns

Ferns unfurl like clumsy dancers,
With muddy boots and silly prancers.
They rustle jokes in the morning light,
Twisting and turning, oh what a sight!

A laughing brook sings the tune,
While frogs croak in a playful swoon.
With every leap and bound they take,
Together they cause the ground to shake.

Verses in the Patch of Sunshine

Sunbeams tickle tiny toes,
While daisies wear their funny clothes.
A ladybug with spots so bright,
Rolls around in pure delight.

Butterflies giggle in the breeze,
Doodling dreams upon the leaves.
Gathering laughter, full of cheer,
As they sway, year after year.

Echoing Heartbeats of the Wild

The trees whisper in silly rhymes,
Echoing secrets through the times.
An owl hoots with a cheeky grin,
As chipmunks tease, let the games begin!

A porcupine juggles with ease,
While raccoons play tricks for a tease.
Nature's jesters, they play all day,
In a silly, charming, wild ballet.

Ballads of the Hidden Glade

In the glade where the squirrels play,
They hide acorns in a silly way.
A chipmunk sings with a high-pitched cheer,
While rabbits hop, spreading joy, not fear.

Leaves tickle toes, a gentle tease,
As whispers float on a sweet, warm breeze.
A fox in a hat prances by with flair,
Claiming he's the best dancer—do beware!

Mushrooms giggle by the shady stream,
Casting shadows in a whimsical dream.
The crickets join with a tap-tap-tap,
As the owls chuckle, caught in a nap.

So come, dear friend, hear the laughter soar,
As we dance through this glade, hearts rich in lore.
With every twist, every joyful chime,
We weave our own tales, like a funny rhyme.

Shadows Dance with Rhythm

Underneath the moon's silver glare,
The shadows waltz without a care.
A hedgehog leads with a tiny spin,
While the fireflies flash, inviting a grin.

Branches sway to a melodic sweep,
As night creatures join from their dreamy sleep.
The badger shimmies with humorous grace,
Step aside, he says, let's quicken the pace!

The owl hoots as he tries to clap,
But winds through feathers, causing a flap.
Beneath tall trees standing so grand,
Nature's mirth brings the whole crowd to stand.

With laughter ringing through night's embrace,
Every shadow finds their own place.
In this rhythm, the wild is alive,
Join the dance, where the silly thrive!

Secrets Written in Bark

On ancient trees, tales swirl with glee,
With carvings of hearts and a mischievous bee.
A raccoon paints with a brush of mud,
While squirrels chatter, spreading the crud.

In crevices, whispers of past frolics dwell,
With lotus flowers that giggle and swell.
A wise old turtle shares jokes of old,
As laughter in nature's hands is boldly told.

The woodpecker taps, inventing a beat,
The groundhogs join, tapping their feet.
With giggles trapped in the knots and nooks,
The woods become pages of funny books.

So read closely, with eyes wide and bright,
The bark has stories of delight at night.
In the heart of the grove, merriment sparks,
As we dance through life and know all the quarks!

Woodland Melodies in the Mist

Amidst the fog that twirls like a waltz,
The leaves play tunes, and nothing exalts.
Frogs croak choirs, each puffing their chest,
Announcing a concert they find quite the best.

The moon peeks through, a curious chap,
As the raccoons giggle, taking a nap.
Amid the fun, there's a sprightly hare,
Dancing around as if he's got flair.

Every creature joins, a whimsical fest,
Where the merry toads sing of peace and jest.
With mushrooms as seats and moss as a rug,
They bounce and they cheer, giving life a shrug.

In the misty night where the wild things play,
Laughter bubbles in a delightful way.
So sway with the night, let worries grow dim,
Join the woodland choir, embrace every whim!

Nature's Chorus in Bloom

The trees wear hats of leafy green,
Squirrels plot, what a scene!
A rabbit hops in quite a rush,
Chasing shadows, oh what a hush.

The birds debate their morning song,
While ants march by, all day long.
A skunk does a dance, oh what a sight,
Promising folks he'll keep it light.

Sunbeams peek, like giggles in the air,
As bushes gossip with flair.
A frog croaks, thinking it's a tune,
Dancing under the light of the moon.

Nature calls, it's a silly game,
Where every critter has a name.
From the tiny bug, to the wise old owl,
In this forest, laughter's on the prowl.

Sonnet of the Wandering Breeze

A breeze blows in with a playful sway,
Twirling leaves like kids at play.
It tickles noses, ruffles hats,
As flowers chuckle at silly spats.

With whispers soft and pokes so light,
It teases bees that bloom with spite.
A leaf slips down, what bold finesse,
While a snail grins in his slow duress.

The wind plays tag with birds up high,
While shadows stretch, and giggles fly.
A twig snaps loud, a startled croak,
As laughter echoes through the oak.

So let us join this breezy fun,
Fluttering hearts like rays of sun.
A symphony of giggles grace,
In every corner of this place.

The Sylvan Symphony

In woods where giggles dance and twirl,
 Each critter wears a friendly swirl.
A raccoon appears with a chef's white hat,
 Baking pies with a swoosh and spat.

Squirrels strum on branches tight,
 Jamming tunes till far too late at night.
 Fungi tap their little feet,
 While fireflies flash a disco beat.

A deer prances with quite the flair,
 Winking at a fox with tousled hair.
 Bees buzz out a quirky hum,
 While trees join in with a funky drum.

The moon's a spotlight on this grand show,
 Where laughter bubbles, free to flow.
 In this grove, wits intertwine,
 Creating rhythms, oh divine!

Rhapsody of Roots and Branches

Beneath the roots, a party brews,
With worms, and snails, in funky shoes.
Mice tell tales of cheese and grace,
While beetles boast of speed in pace.

Tall branches sway, like quips in flight,
A crow jests low, oh what a sight.
With whispers shared among the leaves,
Silly secrets nature weaves.

Amidst the trunks, a dance unfolds,
As laughter echoes, rich like gold.
A chipmunk throws a nutty pun,
While nature grins, oh what fun!

From every nook, joy takes its stance,
In this wood, we find our chance.
To laugh with friends under the sun,
With roots and branches, life's a run!

Murmurs in the Breezy Glade

A squirrel stole my sandwich, oh what a day!
He ran up a tree, I had nothing to say.
The birds laughed along, in their feathery suits,
Chirping their jokes while I searched for my roots.

A frog croaked a tune, with a twist in its leap,
While a caterpillar giggled, not losing its sleep.
They hosted a dance, with all the bugs near,
I stumbled and tripped, oh dear, my dear!

The breeze whispered softly, with a chuckle so low,
As I joined in their frolic, feeling quite slow.
With crickets providing a rhythmic encore,
I jumbled my steps, fell flat on the floor!

But laughter prevailed as the sun waved goodbye,
The hedgehogs all snickered, but I couldn't quite fly.
In the glade where I fumbled and tried to disguise,
Nature taught me that fun wears the best size!

Vibrations of the Well-Worn Path

On the path where I walked, two ants shared a snack,
  I stopped for a moment, wore my best look back.
  They chuckled and chattered, acting quite sly,
    I felt like a giant, just passing them by.

A rabbit, quite dapper, with a top hat so neat,
  Told me that races were on in the street.
He hopped and he bobbed, with a wink and a grin,
We raced down the trail, but I knew he would win!

The trees wrapped their arms 'round a giggling breeze,
  While mushrooms conspired to shake all my keys.
  They whispered of secrets, in colors so bright,
  I danced with a fungus till the fall of the night.

As shadows grew long, my adventure would end,
  I waved at the critters, every foe and friend.
  With laughter encircling all creatures I met,
    I left with a smile, and not one regret!

Embracing the Nature's Sonnet

A porcupine pondered, penning poems for fun,
While fireflies twinkled, outshining the sun.
I asked for advice, but they just blinked bright,
One said, "Be yourself, in the dark or the light!"

The fox in his vest, with a monocle set,
Spoke wise words like fortune cookies I'd get.
He hinted at treasures, all hidden around,
From acorns to berries, the best deals abound!

A raccoon was juggling, oh what a sight,
With cups on his paws and stars shining bright.
I offered to join, but he just laughed loud,
Said, "Stick to the singing; it's what makes you proud!"

So under the stars, we created a tale,
With giggles and rhymes flowing soft on the trail.
Nature's own sonnet, full of twists and turns,
In a world made of wonders, it's laughter that burns!

Lyrical Echoes from Enchanted Thickets

In shadows of thickets, a tune was composed,
By owls who wore glasses, and frogs who all dozed.
The echoes danced round with a whimsical cheer,
While raccoons played tambourines, never in fear.

A hedgehog named Benny spun tales of delight,
He recited his stories, from morning till night.
While turtles all cheered, with their heads stuck in shells,
They sang out their compliments; oh how it swells!

The whispers grew louder, with each passing breeze,
As elves in the bushes shared gossip with ease.
I jumped in to join, but tripped on a root,
Landed right in mud, oh what a big hoot!

Yet laughter ensued, from thickets so dense,
Where fun came alive, making total sense.
In enchanted surrounds, tales spun like the vine,
Echoes of joy, in this woodland divine!

Ballads of the Wandering Deer

A deer with a hat, quite dapper and neat,
Danced in the woods on two little feet.
He twirled with a squirrel, oh what a sight,
While echoing giggles lit up the night.

The trees took a chuckle, the leaves joined along,
As they listened and clapped to this silly song.
A rabbit with boots hopped in for some fun,
While drawing the laughter from everyone.

They pranced through the ferns, a motley parade,
With a tap-dancing frog who was quite unafraid.
A chorus erupted, all critters in tow,
While the moon laughed aloud, casting shadows below.

So under the stars, they'd frolic and play,
With humor and joy lighting up the way.
The deer in his hat took a bow with a grin,
As the forest's own laughter became their hymn.

Serenade of the Silver Moonlight

In moonlight so bright, the snails did a dance,
They twirled on their shells, a whimsical chance.
With a wink and a nudge, they prompted the frogs,
To join in the revel with smiles and hugs.

A hedgehog in spectacles joined in the spree,
Reciting some poetry under a tree.
His words were absurd, made everyone laugh,
As he struggled to read from a dusty old half.

The fireflies sparkled, like gems in the air,
As the critters crowded, without a care.
With laughter and stories, they spun through the night,
In a moonlit soiree, everything felt right.

So let the snails glide, and let frogs sing too,
With laughter so bright, the night feels anew.
In shimmering joy, they chat and they mime,
While the silver moon bathes them, dripping with rhyme.

Whispers Beneath the Bark

Beneath the thick bark, the beetles convened,
To gossip and giggle, their laughter was green.
A gossiping tree said a squirrel had stashed,
A nut in a sock, and the critters all gasped!

A wise owl blinked with an eyebrow raised high,
While mice took a note, never shy to pry.
They crafted a plan, oh the tales they would spin,
For treetop parades with a click and a grin!

The fox dressed in plaid caused a stir with his flair,
He pranced through the bushes, they doubted his care.
While shadows were dancing, wild stories took flight,
As the whispers grew rowdy, deep into night.

So gathered the creatures with secrets to share,
While laughter and nudges filled breezes of air.
With whispers so sweet, they kept each other stark,
In this forest of tales, beneath all the bark.

Chimes of the Buoyant Brook

The brook gurgled softly, its voice filled with glee,
As tadpoles played hopscotch with all of the leaves.
A fish with a mustache proclaimed he could sing,
While the frogs croaked along, adding their zing.

The rocks made a rhythm, a clap and a cheer,
While snails lined the banks and all stopped to hear.
With ripples and splashes, the laughter would swell,
As the water bugs twirled, doing splendidly well.

A turtle, quite festive, wore shades and a grin,
Declaring a party, where fun would begin.
They'd dance on the pebbles, spin tales of the past,
While the brook bubbled joy, a spell that would last.

So let the stream giggle, and let the wind sway,
With tales of adventure, they'll dance every day.
For the water knows magic, in charming delight,
Where chimes of the brook make the world feel just right.

Whispers Beneath the Canopy

Squirrels chatter with glee,
Wiggling their tails with flair.
Beneath the leafy canopy,
They dance without a care.

Birds dive and swoop with zest,
Cracking jokes in the sky.
A wise old owl joins the fest,
With a wink and a sly eye.

Roots tickle in the damp ground,
As giggles bounce from the trees.
Nature's laughter all around,
A comedy of leaves and bees.

So come, oh friend, let's explore,
Where whimsy meets the breeze.
With every step, we'll laugh some more,
In this land of playful trees.

Echoes Among the Trees

What's that rustle? Who's that there?
A rabbit with a top hat on!
He tiptoes light without a care,
While singing the silliest song.

A hedgehog juggles acorns bright,
As foxes clap with delight.
The sun sets, oh what a sight,
With shadows joining in the fight.

Laughter bounces, echoing clear,
Through trunks that nod in joy.
A mischief of creatures, full of cheer,
Turn the night into a ploy.

So join the rhythm of this place,
Where giggles echo true.
With every hop and silly race,
The woods become a zoo!

Verses of the Verdant Grove

In the grove where daisies bloom,
A bear rides a tricycle slow.
His friends all gather, loud with zoom,
To cheer him on and shout, "Go!"

Gnarled limbs twist like a ballet,
As critters prance in the sun.
A raccoon leads a zany sway,
And all the forest joins the fun.

With every rustle the mischief grows,
A symphony of cows and sheep.
They moo and baa as the wind blows,
In harmony, they leap and creep.

The sun dips low, the moon sparks light,
We'll rhyme until the stars appear.
In this grove, the mood is bright,
Filled with laughter, joy, and cheer.

Starlit Paths of Lyrical Dreams

Upon a path where starlight glows,
A frog in a tux takes the lead.
He croaks a tune, and everyone knows,
It's time to dance and take heed.

Fireflies twinkle like tiny stars,
While turtles tap with a beat.
Together they form a band from afar,
Creating music oh so sweet.

Each corner hides a silly surprise,
A deer with glasses and flair.
With laughter echoing to the skies,
They paint the night with great care.

So let's step lightly on this glow,
And join the merry dream team.
With each little giggle, our spirits will grow,
In these starlit paths of gleam.

Echoes of the Hidden Grove

A squirrel in a tiny hat,
Sips acorn tea while on a mat.
A rabbit twirls with great delight,
As fireflies dress up for the night.

A turtle sings a quirky tune,
To the rhythm of the moon.
A fox joins in with clever puns,
They laugh and dance beneath the suns.

A wise old owl with spectacles,
Recites his tales of tentacles.
While shimm'ring leaves in whispers say,
"Join our frolic, it's a play!"

So here in giggles, we do sing,
Of crazy tales and silly things.
Where nature's laughter fills the space,
In our grove of silly grace.

Serenade of the Wildwood

A raccoon plays a tiny lute,
As chipmunks start to dance and hoot.
The brook joins in with splashes bright,
While branches sway with pure delight.

A deer attempts a clumsy waltz,
And stumbles over nature's faults.
The owls just nod their heads and grin,
At this chaotic forest spin.

The daisies giggle in the breeze,
As frogs croak out their symphonies.
The sun sets down like a jelly roll,
While stars peek in to take their stroll.

With each new note, the wildwood sways,
In harmony on silly days.
Let's sing and dance, both young and old,
Our nature's tale will soon unfold.

Sonnet of the Secret Glade

A hedgehog dons a velvet cloak,
While mushrooms laugh and slyly poke.
The breezes whisper silly lore,
As tricksy pixies start to soar.

A pheasant struts in splendid shoes,
And sings the latest forest blues.
The ferns are swaying, not a care,
In this glade, fun's everywhere!

A badger plays a game of chess,
With bee and flower, no more, no less.
The sun peeks in with cheeky rays,
To join our giggles and our plays.

So let's rejoice in this sweet glade,
Where laughter rolls and smiles are made.
Unruly tales from brave and bold,
Dance through the forest, bright and gold.

Rhythms of the Verdant Thicket

In thickets thick with laughs and sighs,
A parrot mimics all the lies.
A snake that slithers sings the blues,
While crickets chirp their silly news.

A caterpillar wears a tie,
And dreams of wings to fly up high.
The bushes giggle, swaying slow,
As rabbits hop and steal the show.

The trees play tricks with wayward vines,
Creating dances with their lines.
While ants march on in funny boots,
With little caps and tiny flutes.

In this thicket, joy's the norm,
Where nature's jests become the charm.
With every chuckle, life ignites,
In rhythms of the wild delights.

Verses from the Mossy Floor

Squirrels gossip in the trees,
About acorns, nuts, and bees.
A raccoon winks with a smirk,
Saying, 'I plan to go berserk!'

Mossy floor, a trampoline,
Jumping jokes unseen, I mean.
Frogs wear crowns, jump around,
King of nonsense, truly crowned!

Toads sing hymns with goofy pride,
While fireflies flit and glide.
Laughter echoes, wild and free,
In this forest jubilee!

Beneath the pines, we share a grin,
Who knew fun could grow within?
So come along, don't be shy,
In this woodland, laughter flies!

Reflections in the Woodland Stream

Glittering fish with flashy scales,
Crack wise like woodland tales.
'Why swim straight?' a minnow jokes,
'I prefer my life in strokes!'

Ducklings quack with silly glee,
Making waves, a jubilee.
'Catch me if you can!' they shout,
Splashes flying all about!

A turtle grins, taking it slow,
Says, 'I'm the king of take-it-low!'
Mirror laughs with every wave,
As the forest tries to behave.

Ripples dance with shiny charm,
Wobbling like a cozy farm.
In this stream, we wade with cheer,
All our worries disappear!

Dreams of the Sylvan Realm

Trees wear hats made of green,
A jolly sight like you've never seen.
Owls in specs, wise and bright,
Debate the logic of day and night.

Beetles parade in tiny cars,
Zooming past under twinkling stars.
'I'm late for tea,' a ladybug shouts,
While a caterpillar grins and pouts.

The breeze brings whispers and fun,
'Let's race!' the mushrooms shout, one by one.
With giggles cascading through the trees,
Even the branches sway with these.

In this dreamland, jokes abound,
Where every rustle lifts the sound.
Join us, dear friend, in this place,
Where laughter leaves a cheerful trace!

Enchanted by Dappled Light

Sunbeams dance on the forest floor,
Each ray a giggle, who could ask for more?
A shadow twirls, come take a peek,
And a gnome waves with a silly squeak.

Fairies throw a sparkling ball,
With toadstools as chairs, oh, what a sprawl!
'Shake a leg!' the mushrooms say,
As they jive the night away!

A fox joins in, with a hopping twist,
'Dance with me, you can't resist!'
While squirrels cheer from the high-heeled trees,
Chanting their rhymes with energetic ease.

In this light, shadows giggle,
Every moment just makes you wiggle.
So let's play, let's dance, let's sing,
In this shimmering world, joy is king!

The Language of the Ancient Underbrush

In whispers soft beneath our feet,
The plants debate the day's defeat.
A squirrel takes the leading role,
While daisies giggle, losing control.

The mushrooms dance in lively pairs,
While crickets tune their tiny snares.
A hedgehog writes with pride and glee,
His tales of snacks' most glorious spree.

The leaves are gossiping, don't you know?
About the acorn's hat and its funny flow.
A beetle's boast of weighty pride,
Leaves us all rolling, eyes open wide.

So next time you roam where wild things hide,
Join the chatter, let laughter abide.
For nature's jesters are always around,
In the ancient underbrush, humor's found.

Symphony of Ancient Trunks

Tall trees gather and bang their heads,
With woody laughter, they share some spreads.
The owls play drums with a whoot and a flap,
While raccoons wear ties, ready for a nap.

Birds chirp songs of old romance,
As squirrels do their acorn dance.
The branches sway in humorous hum,
While lost in thought, a deer goes 'duh!'

Whispers echo from bark so wise,
A gray old tree did roll its eyes.
'Oh, those youngsters!' he chuckles aloud,
As the wind joins in, dancing, proud.

So, gather close to hear the show,
With trunks that tap, and leaves that blow.
In laughter, all the creatures merge,
In symphonies that make the heart surge.

The Dreamweaver of Rustic Leaves

A leaf fell down, a hat for a bug,
That shimmies and shakes with a happy shrug.
Mice roll by on a woodland cruise,
In shoes made of bark, with silly hues.

Underneath the branches, a story unwinds,
Of a turtle with dreams and silly designs.
He wished for wings, just for a day,
To fly with the birds and then drift away.

The sun giggles down through a leafy embrace,
As shadows play tag in a fanciful race.
A snail yells out, "Catch me if you dare!"
While butterflies twirl without a care.

In this playful realm where magic is real,
The dreamweaver weaves the day's bright appeal.
So let your heart leap, in laughter, entwine,
Among rustic leaves, where fun will align.

Lullabies of the Leafy Realm

In a tree wearing pajamas, so bright,
A squirrel taught a raccoon to take flight.
They flipped and they flopped, in pure delight,
The branches shook as they giggled with might.

A hedgehog joined in with a drum made of leaves,
While bunnies danced round like a bunch of reprieves.
They sang to the moon, oh how it perceives,
Nature's own lullaby, everyone believes.

A parrot in shades wore a hat made of vines,
He crooned silly songs, wrote poetic designs.
With each little verse, all the forest aligns,
As laughter bubbles up through the tall leafy pines.

So join the ruckus, come play by the tree,
Where all the odd creatures share joyfully.
In this leafy realm, you'll always be free,
To laugh with the critters in each melody!

Ode to the Enchanted Woods

Beneath a mushroom, a dance party brews,
Fairies serve cupcakes while gnomes tie their shoes.
With twirling and swirling, they sing out their blues,
Each step a giggle, in vibrant hues.

The owls are the DJs, they hoot out the beat,
A hedgehog in shades has dance moves quite sweet.
While turtles snap photos, a whole lot of heat,
And critters converge for the grandest retreat.

Beneath the tall trees, a chorus takes flight,\nAs chipmunks tap dance, it's quite the sight!
With rhymes and with laughter that stretch deep at night,
These woods are enchanted, and oh, what a light!

For mischief and magic, just step right inside,
Where chuckles and chortles at every turn reside.
In this joyful place, let your worries slide,
For each moment here is a fun-filled ride!

Harmonies of the Wilderness

With a croak and a chirp, the frogs gather round,
In the orchestra pit, where the funny sounds drown.
A raccoon in a tux plays the best in town,
While fireflies twinkle, a sparkly crown.

The owls keep the rhythm, tapping their beaks,
While chipmunks add jazz with their hilarious tweaks.
The bear does the cha-cha, though balance it seeks,
As laughter erupts, and joy simply peaks.

The wildflowers sway, to the music they hum,
A parade of nutty beats, making all the fun.
A band of raccoons with a roll and a strum,
In this wild wilderness, joyous hearts will not glum.

So gather your friends, let's dance 'neath the stars,
With melodies weaving our dreams from afar.
In harmonies wild, we'll forget all our scars,
For this is the realm where the laughter bizarre!

Chants by the Tranquil Stream

By the stream, the frogs chant out loud and clear,
A fish with a mustache joins in with no fear.
"Let's start a band!" says a brave little deer,
And soon there's a chorus of giggles and cheer.

A turtle in glasses recites silly rhymes,
While the dragonflies buzz with their rhythmic chimes.
Each creature awakens, as nature unwinds,
And creativity flows, as laughter climbs.

With a splash and a plop, they join in the fun,
Even shy little hedgehogs come out for a run.
They twirl and they flip, basking under the sun,
In the rhythm of water, joy's never undone.

So come to the stream where the antics are bright,
Let the creatures inspire, and let spirits take flight.
With a smile and a song, everything feels right,
In this tranquil paradise, all day and all night!

Tales from the Sheltering Canopy

Squirrels gossip near the tree,
Raccoons laughing with such glee.
They trade their nuts for juicy pies,
While owls hoot loud with sleepy sighs.

A rabbit wears a silly hat,
Dancing round a sleeping cat.
Frogs in tuxedos croak and prance,
Each blushing flower joins the dance.

The ants march by, a marching band,
With acorn drums and sticks in hand.
They stumble, trip, and fall in rows,
As laughter rings where the wild wind blows.

Lizards lounge beneath the shade,
Boasting tales of charades played.
In this realm of giggles bright,
The woods come alive with sheer delight.

Cadence of the Starlit Glade

Fireflies twinkle with finesse,
Dancing round in light's caress.
Crickets chirp a nightly tune,
As raccoons steal a silver spoon.

Bats swoop low with quiet grace,
While owls play hide-and-seek in space.
A hedgehog's wiggle shakes the leaves,
And every branch the mischief weaves.

The moon's a jester, quite absurd,
Tickling trees with a fluffy bird.
Tales of laughter echo clear,
A symphony the heart holds dear.

Badgers bumble with a trot,
In shadows where the laughs are caught.
With giggles shared overhead,
The woods are known for pranks well bred.

The Muse of the Overhanging Vines

Vines dangle down like silly strings,
Tying up all the forest flings.
Monkeys swing with joyful cheer,
While random plants lend an ear.

A silly lizard wears a crown,
Sure he'll win if a race goes down.
The butterflies toss colors bright,
Whispering secrets through the night.

Tangled limbs and hidden sights,
Crackling laughter under starlight.
Nuts rolled down a little hill,
The forest echoes, "What a thrill!"

A porcupine hums a tune,
With sticks and stones that's bound to croon.
In this wild and funny scene,
Life's but a jest, a merry green.

Odes to the Sylvan Shadows

Shadows whisper silly dreams,
As nocturnal critters scheme.
Chasing fireflies, bats take flight,
In a dance of pure delight.

A turtle slides past with a grin,
While shadows laugh and tumble in.
The mushrooms giggle, squishy traits,
Tickling toes of passing mates.

A band of mice in coats of gray,
Singing songs of yesterday.
Each note a chuckle, cheeky cheer,
Through every nook, the laughter's near.

Beneath the winking stars of blue,
The forest knows just what to do.
With every shadow, jest and rhyme,
It's a playful world, all in good time.

Ballad of the Wandering Path

Lost my shoe on trail so wide,
A bear sat down while I just cried.
He grinned at me, I swear he smiled,
I thought, 'This forest is quite wild!'

Twigs and branches, oh what a snare,
My hat got caught in a low-hanging hair.
I danced like a fool, laughing in glee,
Who knew the woods were a circus, you see?

A squirrel scolded me, what a fuss,
'You're here for fun, but you're making a mess!'
With pine cones flying, I quickly ducked,
Who knew the critters could get this ruck(ed)?

Next time I'll tread, with shoe firmly tied,
And avoid the bear who once mocked my pride.
Though every trip brings its own silly claim,
This wandering path will never be the same!

Chants of the Ancient Roots

Ancient trees whisper jokes to the sky,
Their twisted branches have learned to fly.
A raccoon joins in, giggling with glee,
Says, 'I've got the best punchline, wait and see!'

Roots like noodles, tangled and spry,
Tripping over them makes my spirits fly.
The owls hoot loud, their wise eyes twinkling,
While I juggle acorns, my laughter crinkling.

A fox in a bowtie struts in a dance,
'This is my gala! Come take a chance!'
With woodland critters all dressed up bright,
Who knew fungi could throw such delight?

With each chant and cheer, the forest comes alive,
An ancient jest that helps us thrive.
In the company of roots, so silly and grand,
We'll laugh through the trees, hand in hand!

Melodies Beneath the Boughs

Beneath the boughs, where shadows play,
Chirping cricket bands brighten the day.
Beetles tap dance, it's quite the show,
With mushrooms to cheer, they steal the glow.

Pine needle strings, a harp in the breeze,
With melodies woven from the squirrels' tease.
Frogs join the chorus, croaking in tune,
While fireflies blink to a jazzy moon.

'Hey there, buddy!' a woodpecker sings,
'Is that your hat? It's now for the king!'
Laughter erupts at such goofy sight,
As branches sway gently, weaving delight.

So let's celebrate this forest spree,
Where whimsy abounds and all can be free.
With tunes and giggles, we sway and sway,
Beneath the boughs, forever we'll stay!

Harmonies of the Leafy Aisle

Down the leafy aisle, the bees start to hum,
While rabbits play drums with their clever thrum.
A hedgehog jives on a sparkly stone,
I can't help but laugh — this place feels like home.

Leaves flutter like dancers, a vibrant ballet,
While misty clouds giggle and float far away.
Every rustle and whisper's a tune of its own,
Even the squirrels seem to carry the tone.

Twisting and turning, we skip and we sway,
Mice crash the party, in their own funny way.
With laughter and joy, we join the parade,
In this leafy aisle where silliness is made.

So grab your friends, come join the light,
With melodies soaring into the night.
In the heart of the green, where giggles compile,
We find our harmony down the leafy aisle!

Twilight Whispers of the Wandering Soul

In the shadows, we trip and tumble,
Yet giggles escape as we quietly fumble.
Owls hoot in sync with our little dance,
While fireflies join in, given the chance.

Branches bend low, snagging our hats,
We dodge rogue squirrels and playful spats.
The moon peeks shyly, a curious friend,
As we prank the night till the laughter can blend.

The path twists around like a silly joke,
With whispers of mischief from each little oak.
Encountering foxes who wink and tease,
As we laugh till we cry, watching them freeze.

Twilight dangles stars as we jump and spin,
Chasing our shadows, we feel like kin.
The woods are alive with our joy and jest,
In whispers of twilight, we feel truly blessed.

Harmonies of the Dancing Petals

Amidst flowers waltzing, we strut and sway,
With stumbles and giggles, we brighten the day.
Bees buzz with laughter, a honeyed tune,
While petals pirouette, float and balloon.

We bump into daisies, they scatter in fright,
As we jiggle and jive, creating delight.
With each step we take, a chorus of cheer,
Nature's own orphans, we conquer our fear.

A napkin of leaves wraps our sudden fall,
While butterflies snicker, oh, what a ball!
The grass is our stage; it feels quite absurd,
As we leap and we whirl, life's comedy stirred.

In laughter we drown, in petals we float,
With giggles as music, our hearts fill the note.
Dancing through meadows, we make quite a scene,
In the symphony of blooms, we reign as the queen.

A Tapestry of Leafy Verses

In a quilt of green, we fashion our rhyme,
With squirrelly side quests, all too sublime.
Leaves rustle softly, giggling with glee,
As we search for the words that whisper and tease.

We pen down our echoes, crumpled in jest,
With acorns as ink, we try our best.
"A tree doesn't giggle," we boldly declared,
Yet the branches chuckle, and we can't be spared.

The sun winks atop with a mischievous glow,
Bidding farewell to the day's lively show.
Each verse a vine, wrapping us tight,
In a tapestry spun under dimming twilight.

So let's dance with the shadows, compose a new tune,
Where laughter and words are a joyful festoon.
As the leaves rustle 'round, we'll pen our last line,
In this leafy adventure, oh, isn't it fine?

The Quivering Silence of the Night

In the stillness we linger, hearts full of dreams,
While the darkness giggles with faint silver beams.
A rustle draws attention, a clumsy deer,
More startled than us, but oh, how we cheer!

The moon's a big cheese; it lets out a grin,
Whispering secrets to the critters within.
We hold our breaths tight, with mischief ablaze,
In a game of shadow, we dance and we blaze.

A chorus of crickets leads the grand song,
While a wise old owl shakes his head, "What's wrong?"
"Nothing!" we yell, as we fall with a thump,
The quivering silence burst forth with a jump.

So we embrace the night with all of our glee,
In this circus of stars, wild and free.
With laughter painting silence, the jokes take flight,
In the quivering silence, we reign through the night.

Whimsy of the Woodland Creatures

Squirrels in hats, oh what a sight,
Dancing around in the pale moonlight.
They swap their acorns for candy bars,
Singing songs of raccoon guitars.

A fox wears glasses, quite out of place,
Reading a novel with a fuzzy face.
While rabbits hop in matching shoes,
Painting their nails in vibrant hues.

The owl attempts a stand-up routine,
Yet nobody laughs; oh, what a scene!
Even the hedgehog rolls his eyes,
Saying, "That joke? Just a bunch of lies!"

With butterflies twirling like ballerinas,
Nature's party has no subpoenas.
Whimsy abounds, let laughter soar,
In this woodland where silliness roars!

Chronicles of the Majestic Oaks

Beneath the oaks so grand and tall,
The squirrels plan their acorn brawl.
"Mine is bigger!" Young Chipmunk declares,
As they giggle over their leafy lairs.

The elder tree sighs, "Oh what a fuss!
Just share your stash, there's plenty for us!"
The wind whispers secrets to the grass,
Playing pranks like a cheeky class.

Mice in tuxedos wander the scene,
Hosting tea parties, so very keen.
A raccoon sneaks in, steals a scone,
Leaving the guests to squawk and moan!

Yet laughter erupts in this dappled shade,
As dance-offs break out, fun never fades.
In tales of trees, humor entwines,
In their embrace, joy brightly shines!

Poetics of the Forest Floor

On the floor of leaves, a party unfolds,
With mushrooms that chatter, and tales that are bold.
The grasshoppers croon, writing ballads anew,
While ants do the conga, all covered in dew.

A snail with a trumpet plays jazzy tunes,
While crickets sync up and dance 'neath the moons.
Twirling and whirling, oh what a blast,
Each creature's a star, at least for the cast!

A stray cat strolls in, gives a smirk,
Catching the vibe with a lazy perk.
"Amateurs!" it laughs, with a flick of the tail,
Then sprawls out to sunbathe without any fail!

But as dusk approaches, the fun won't stop,
With glowworms alight, they're ready to hop.
In every nook, a giggle hides,
As poetics bloom where the wild humor abides.

Stanzas from the Pine-Scented Dusk

As twilight drapes its soft, cozy gown,
Creatures in pajamas parade through the town.
The porcupine plays its big bass guitar,
While skunks add the beat—oh, how bizarre!

Chirps from the frogs set the rhythm quite right,
Making all critters bounce and ignite.
A hedgehog DJ spins records around,
While fireflies illuminate this sound.

"Who wants hot dogs?" a raven screeches loud,
With a grin and a wink, it gathers a crowd.
Sassy raccoons with relish and buns,
Serve meals with flair; oh, what funny runs!

As night grows thick, the laughter resounds,
With selfies and stories, they spin their rounds.
Pine-scented dusk cradles the night,
In this whimsical land, all feels just right!

A Symphony of Celestial Shadows

We danced with squirrels under the trees,
Their acorn hats blown off by a breeze.
The sun peeked through in a playful game,
While laughing leaves whispered our names.

A badger sang out a ditty or two,
With a voice that sounded like a cow on cue.
We clapped our paws and stamped on the ground,
As frogs joined in with a croaky sound.

A rabbit hopped in on a pogo stick,
While snails debated who'd be the quick.
The owls rolled their eyes, their wisdom on show,
"Keep it down!" they hooted, "We're trying to grow!"

With each wooden bench a stage for a show,
The trees were the curtains, the shadows aglow.
We laughed 'til we cried, lost track of the hours,
In our symphony made of amusing flowers.

Daydreams in the Sunlit Hollow

In the hollow where the sunlight beams,
We chased after our wildest dreams.
A chipmunk juggled nuts with flair,
While fireflies danced, unaware of a care.

The tall grass giggled, with secrets to share,
As butterflies plotted to tease the air.
A snail took a leap, 'No time to delay!'
But tripped on a twig and rolled away.

We painted the sky with clouds made of cream,
And drank our lemonade with a splash and a scream.
A hedgehog in sunglasses, looking so cool,
Taught us that sunbathing is really a rule.

With each little laugh, the day felt bright,
In the warm sun's glow, everything felt right.
We gathered the whimsy that danced in the light,
In daydreams alive, oh, what a delight!

The Gentle Sway of Nature's Heart

Beneath the boughs where whispers twirl,
We twirled 'round like a dizzying whirl.
A deer wore a crown made of fern and flower,
While turtles debated who'd climb the tower.

The bees buzzed by, each one in a rush,
They stumbled a bit, oh what a hush!
An owl in the rafters raised an eyebrow,
Muttering, "What's this? Come on, take a bow."

Each leaf's gentle laugh was a marvelous sound,
As we stumbled and tripped on the soft, squishy ground.
The trees cracked a joke that echoed wide,
While mushrooms giggled, refusing to hide.

So we danced and we played, in moments of cheer,
The gentle sway making laughter near.
With nature's embrace and spirit so free,
In each silly moment, we found pure glee!

Chronicles of the Silent Watchers

In the hush of the glen, the watchers convene,
With eyes all aglow, they observe the scene.
A hedgehog in glasses takes notes with delight,
"Did you see that squirrel? What a remarkable sight!"

The rocks sat in silence, wise and profound,
While mushrooms exchanged tales without making a sound.
A dragonfly giggled and took to the sky,
"Let's make this a saga, oh me, oh my!"

The owls sipped tea at the midnight hour,
Commenting on bloom and each flower's power.
"We've seen every act, from the silly to grand,
In this vibrant stage of our enchanted land."

With each manmade chaos and whimsical flare,
The chronicles grow rich as the stories declare.
So here's to the watchers, both bold and bizarre,
Crafting laughter and dreams beneath the stars.

Fables from the Ferns

A squirrel named Ted sold nuts with glee,
He charged the birds a hefty fee.
But when they took flight, oh what a sight!
Ted found himself alone by a tree.

Beneath the ferns, a snail was lost,
He asked for directions, but at what cost?
The toad just croaked, 'Try not to choke!'
And left the slow slug feeling quite crossed.

A hedgehog sought fame in the online space,
With selfies and posts, he thought he'd ace.
But his prickly face made him quite a disgrace,
As likes fell off faster than a race!

And so in the woods, with laughter and cheer,
The animals share their tales year by year.
Each fable is funny, absurdity plenty,
In their leafy retreats, they spread joy with beer!

Refrains of the Rustling Leaves

The breeze sang to flowers, oh what a tune,
It danced with the bees, who swayed to the moon.
One bee took a drink, forgot about work,
And buzzed round a flower, acting like a jerk.

The leaves whispered secrets, gossiping shy,
About a fat fox who thought he could fly.
He tried on a kite for a daring escape,
But ended up tangled in a berry grape!

An owl with bad jokes hooted in rhymes,
He told the wise trees he'd run out of times.
With each groan that followed, the forest agreed,
He should stick to the night and give up on the deed.

And so through the branches, the laughter would weave,
Creating sweet music no one could believe.
Rustling with joy, they'd chatter away,
Until the sun's rise marked the start of their play.

Poetry Lingers in the Pines

In the pines, a raccoon had a book of bad rhymes,
He read to his friends, and oh, they had times!
With chuckles and snorts, they fell off their seats,
Each line much worse than last week's tweets.

A pair of wise owls kept hooting in jest,
Claiming their wisdom was surely the best.
But a squirrel named Claire took them to task,
She challenged their knowledge, so what could they ask?

At night by the moon, a critter parade,
With dance moves so silly, they pensively swayed.
The chipmunk did cartwheels, but tripped on a stone,
And landed right next to a gopher's old throne.

Thus laughter would echo, through needles and bark,
As poetry lingered until it grew dark.
In the heart of the pines, with giggles that climb,
A forest of joy sings on every chime.

A Tapestry of Twilight Verses

At dusk a fox wore a top hat of straw,
He fancied himself quite the dapper old law.
But with a sly wink, his hat took a flight,
It soared off his head, much to his delight!

A colorful parrot went shopping for threads,
He dressed like a clown but convinced they were rends.
With feathers a-flutter, he strutted down paths,
While giggling at rabbits and their silly wraths.

The raccoons held meetings in circles of glow,
Deciding whose turn it was next to bestow.
Cajoling and jesting, "Our games never cease!"
Their tapestry bright with laughter and peace.

And twilight enfolds them, a calm in the night,
While verses of humor take wing with delight.
Amongst the tall trees where giggles persist,
They weave a warm quilt, a wonder to list.

The Poetry of Moss and Stone

Mossy blankets on rocks sit tight,
Whispering jokes in the pale moonlight.
Stones giggle softly, in earthy tones,
As squirrels debate with their acorn phones.

The trees catch on with a playful cheer,
Shouting secrets for all nearby to hear.
Laughter echoes through branches with flair,
As rabbits mock dance in the cool night air.

A frog croaks puns from a murky pool,
With dreams of a prince, he plays the fool.
Beneath a shout of a hooting owl,
They tell tall tales with each gleeful growl.

So if you wander where giggles abound,
Join in the fun, make silly sounds.
For in this realm where the wild things play,
The poetry of nature will brighten your day.

Stanzas in the Shade

Under leafy hats, the wise old trees,
Share rhymes that tickle like warm summer breeze.
Each leaf holds a secret, a pun or a joke,
While shadows dance lightly, no need for a cloak.

A chipmunk chimes in with a nutty refrain,
"Don't take life too seriously, it's all just a game!"
The sunbeams nod gently, all smiles and grins,
As flowers reply with their own silly sins.

In the shade, critters practice their lines,
Beavers, woodpeckers, and grand old pines.
They gather for laughter, a little play fight,
And all through the day, they're a marvelous sight.

So linger awhile in this jolly retreat,
Where giggles and stanzas are joyous and sweet.
Embrace the silliness, let your heart sway,
For life is a poem, come join in the play.

Serenades of the Ancient Oaks

Under the gaze of aged, wise oaks,
The air is alive with whimsical jokes.
Their branches sway gently, a rhythmic delight,
To serenades sung through the cool, crisp night.

A squirrel in slippers brings laughter to all,
Twirling around, not afraid of a fall.
With acorns for maracas, he joins in the fun,
As crickets keep tempo, one by one.

The oaks share their stories, a comedic twist,
Of a rascally rabbit who loves to assist.
He could hop and he'd skip, until he fell down,
In a heap full of laughter, instead of a frown.

So find your own place where the fun tends to grow,
Amongst laughing trees, let your spirit glow.
With every old oak and each giggling breeze,
The serenade lives on, putting hearts at ease.

Lyrics Carried on the Wind

Whispers of humor float through the air,
As wind carries tales with an elegant flair.
Each gust sings a song with a lighthearted twist,
Of hedgehogs in bowties and frogs that can't resist.

Dancing through brambles, the breeze shares a rhyme,
Of bees who recite while they sweeten their time.
With flowers in bloom as their bright, buzzing choir,
They turn simple murmurs to joyful satire.

Pathways are lined with the echoes of snickers,
As wily old foxes engage in some bickers.
Between trickster and jest, the forest's alive,
With stories and laughter where mischief can thrive.

So listen intently as the wind spins a tale,
Of antics and joy that will never grow stale.
In this whimsical world where chortles descend,
Find giggles and glee in the lyrics they send.

Cadences of the Nostalgic Trail

A squirrel danced, his tail a plume,
He stole my snack, oh dreadful doom!
With acorns tossed like tiny bombs,
I took a breath and practiced psalms.

The rabbits plotted on their way,
To steal my lunch, then run and play!
But I had snacks still up my sleeve,
And soon they'd find they can't deceive.

The trees all laughed, their branches swayed,
In whispers soft, they all conveyed:
"The joggers trod like clumsy gnomes,
Just hear how every shoe-bump moans!"

I tossed my chips to chipmunks bright,
As they performed a silly flight.
Their furry bodies leapt with glee,
A circus act for all to see!

Ink of the Ancient Sap

A tree once claimed a writer's pen,
And started telling tales again.
With every drop of sap, it wrote,
The stories of a forest vote!

The owls would hoot, the squirrels would cheer,
"More stories, please! We want to hear!"
With messy ink of golden goo,
They wrote of mischief, tried and true.

The stones would laugh, the moss would sigh,
As tales of blobs just floated by.
A dragonfly with sparkly wings,
Composed a tune that always swings!

But when it rained, their papers flew,
While raindrops joined the crazy crew.
Each tale was soaked, the forest groaned,
Yet in their hearts, the laughter honed.

Secret Songs of the Rustic Haven

The frogs began a chorale grand,
With ribbits strong, a concert planned.
A turtle played a shaky tune,
Beneath the glow of silver moon.

The fireflies twinkled, signed the beat,
While crickets tapped their tiny feet.
They gathered close, a merry band,
An orchestra of nature's hand.

The owls sang notes from way up high,
While branches lived their lullaby.
A raccoon's joke made everyone laugh,
As he stole snacks from the silly staff!

The night went on, the music swirled,
A symphony from nature's world.
With secret songs that no one penned,
A rhythm that would never end!

Reverie Beneath Broken Branches

Beneath the branches, dreams took flight,
With whispers soft, in the fading light.
A hedgehog snored, a fox desired,
To build a campfire, inspired!

The mushrooms grinned, they knew the score,
While pixies peeked from behind the door.
They shared their tales of pranks and fun,
While spiders wove their webs, well done.

The wind would chuckle, brushing by,
As snappy plants would never lie.
"Beware the bear, he just eats pies!"
So whispered friends with playful eyes.

But all agreed, the best delight,
Was gathering under stars so bright.
Where laughter rang and bonds took flight,
In dreams we found our heart's ignite.

www.ingramcontent.com/pod-product-compliance
Lightning Source LLC
Chambersburg PA
CBHW071815160426
43209CB00003B/98